THE STAR-SPANGLED BANNER

W9-CAU-522

SCHOLASTIC INC. Cartwheel B·O·O·K·S®

New York   Toronto   London   Auckland   Sydney   Mexico City   New Delhi   Hong Kong   Buenos Aires

Photography credits for *The Star-Spangled Banner*:
Cover: Myrleen F. Cate/PhotoEdit, Long Beach, CA.
Back cover: Owen Franken/Corbis.
Pages: 3: Dennis MacDonald/PhotoEdit; 4: Terry Eggers/Corbis Stock Market; 5: Stone/Getty Images; 6, top left: James P. Blair/Corbis; top right: Joseph Sohm/Corbis; bottom right: Myrleen F. Cate/PhotoEdit; bottom left: Gary Conner/PhotoEdit; 7: Gary Conner/PhotoEdit; 8–9: Stone/Getty Images; 10: Kevin Fleming/Corbis; 11: Stock Montage/SuperStock; 12: A.K.G., Berlin/SuperStock; 13: SuperStock; 14–15: A.K.G., Berlin/SuperStock; 16: Michael Newman/PhotoEdit; 17, top left: SuperStock; top right: Kelly/Mooney Photography/Corbis; bottom right: Joseph Sohm/Corbis; bottom left: Rachel Epstein/PhotoEdit; 18: SuperStock; 19: David Young-Wolff/PhotoEdit; 20: Stone/Getty Images; 21: SuperStock; 22: Joseph Sohm/Corbis; 23: Eye Wire/Getty Images; 24: Robert Brenner/PhotoEdit.

Photo Research by Sarah Longacre

No part of this publication may be reproduced, or stored in a retrieval system, or transmitted in any form or by any means, electronic, mechanical, photocopying, recording, or otherwise, without written permission of the publisher. For information regarding permission, write to Scholastic Inc., Attention: Permissions Department, 557 Broadway, New York, NY 10012.

ISBN 0-439-40767-2

Copyright © 2002 by Scholastic Inc.
All rights reserved. Published by Scholastic Inc.
SCHOLASTIC, CARTWHEEL BOOKS, and associated logos are trademarks and/or registered trademarks of Scholastic Inc.

12 11 10 9 8 7 6 5 4 3 2 1   2 3 4 5 6 7/0

Printed in the U.S.A.   08
First printing, May 2002

O say, can you see,

by the dawn's early light,

What so proudly we hailed

at the twilight's last gleaming?

Whose broad stripes

and bright stars,

through the perilous fight,

O'er the ramparts we watched,
were so gallantly streaming?

And the rockets' red glare,
the bombs bursting in air,

Gave proof through the night

that our flag was still there.

O say, does that star-spangled
banner yet wave

O'er the land of the free

and the home of the brave?

O say, can you see, by the dawn's early light,

What so proudly we hailed at the twilight's last gleaming?

Whose broad stripes and bright stars, through the perilous fight,

O'er the ramparts we watched, were so gallantly streaming?

And the rockets' red glare, the bombs bursting in air,

Gave proof through the night that our flag was still there.

O say, does that star-spangled banner yet wave

O'er the land of the free and the home of the brave?